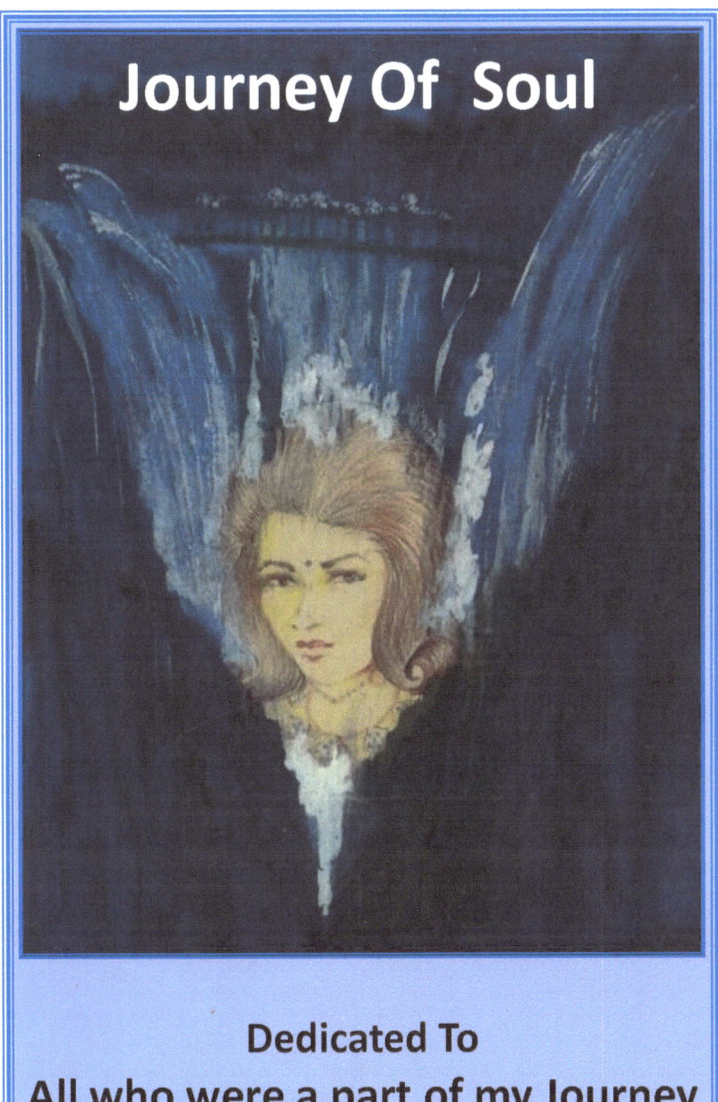

Journey Of Soul

Dedicated To
All who were a part of my Journey

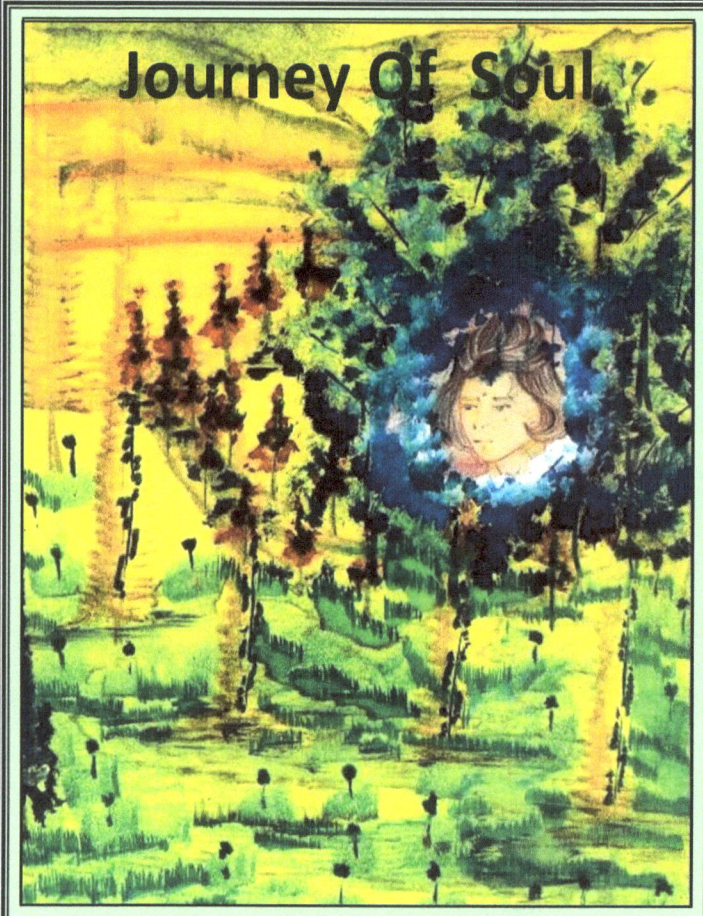

Journey Of Soul

Copyright@ 2016 by Aditya Kumar Daga

About The Book

Collection of my Original Arts. All Arts are Mixed Arts. Medley of not only colors but also of emotions & sketches based on such emotions at different times & different moods. My Own 'Lyrics' & 'Poetries'.

We are at a journey of life. Our emotions not only flowing from heart but also a medleys of emotions of our near and dear ones, emotions of our friends and relatives, emotions of our mentors and preachers. We get sorrowful on the sorrows of others. We get happy on the happiness of others. Why it happens ? As because we get a link of 'Soul'.

We are at a journey of life but at the same time our soul is also at a journey. Sometimes we unexpectedly dreams something amazing , something weird, something like a life story directed by someone on a big screen. All such sub conscious thinking had a deep link with our soul and journey of soul. Without this journey we can never do 'premonitions & Intuitions' 'Research & Explorations' 'Emotions' & 'Tears'.

So I have given an 'Image' of an emotional sensitive female figure to my 'Soul'. It's not a physical appearance but a shadow of myself lingering and lurking over my past foregone days and forgone emotions, relations, dreams, expectations, wishes, hopes and my happiness.

Whenever I close my eyes and go into my subconscious stage I feel distractions, dejections, melancholia, loneliness, despondencies and a very weird feeling of nothingness, blankness, vacuum inside my soul. My heart start succumbing and causing feather like lightness in my body as I have no energy, strength and power to consummate 'present' even a little.

My soul had dreams, had my childhood imaginations, ideas, fancies, had my teen age fantasies, had young age ecstasies, having lingering adulthood, now facing ageing agonies, contemplating premonitions of old age loneliness & melancholia—A journey of soul continuing from my past life, continuing this life any may be continued to the next life. Death is inevitable but journey of soul is immortal & non ending.

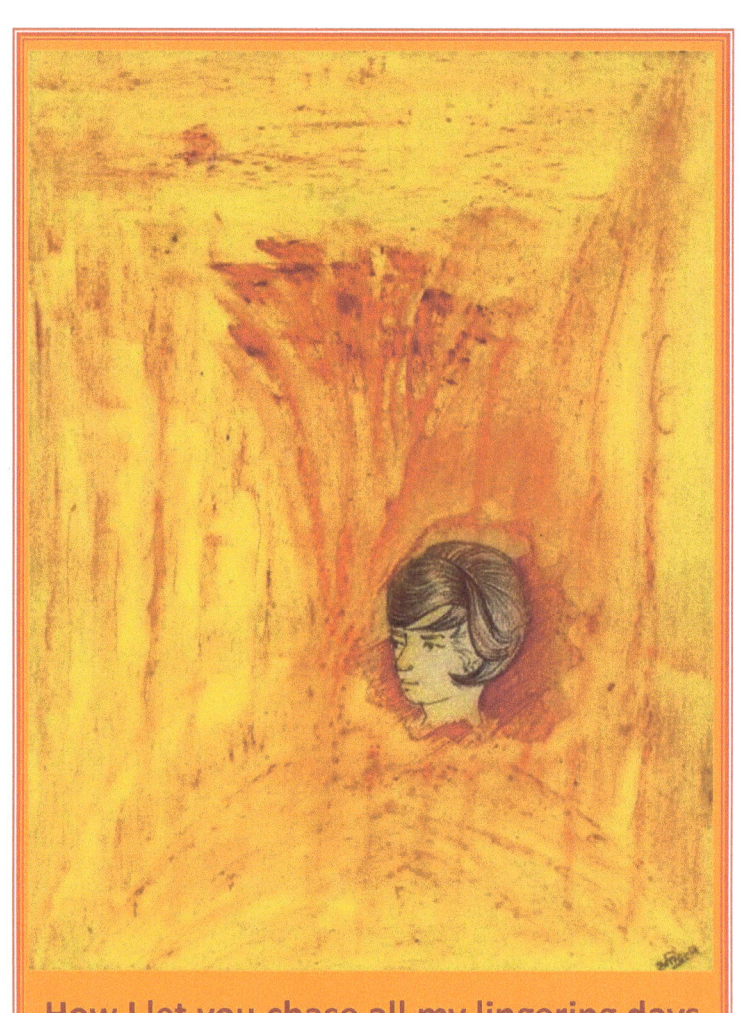

How I let you chase all my lingering days

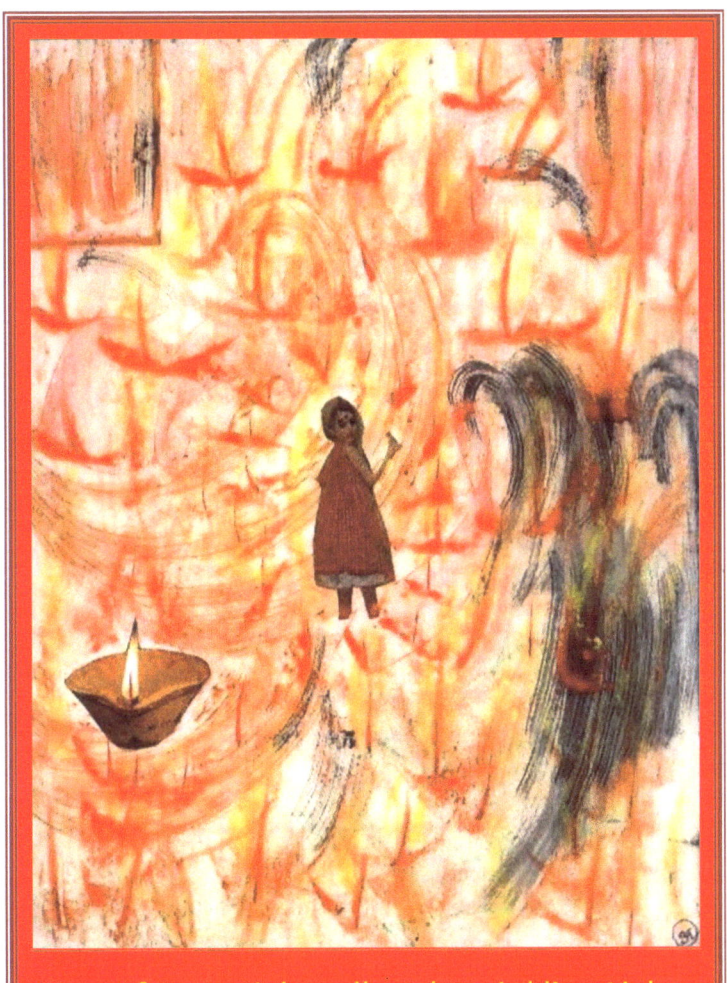

How I forget nights all such twinkling Lights

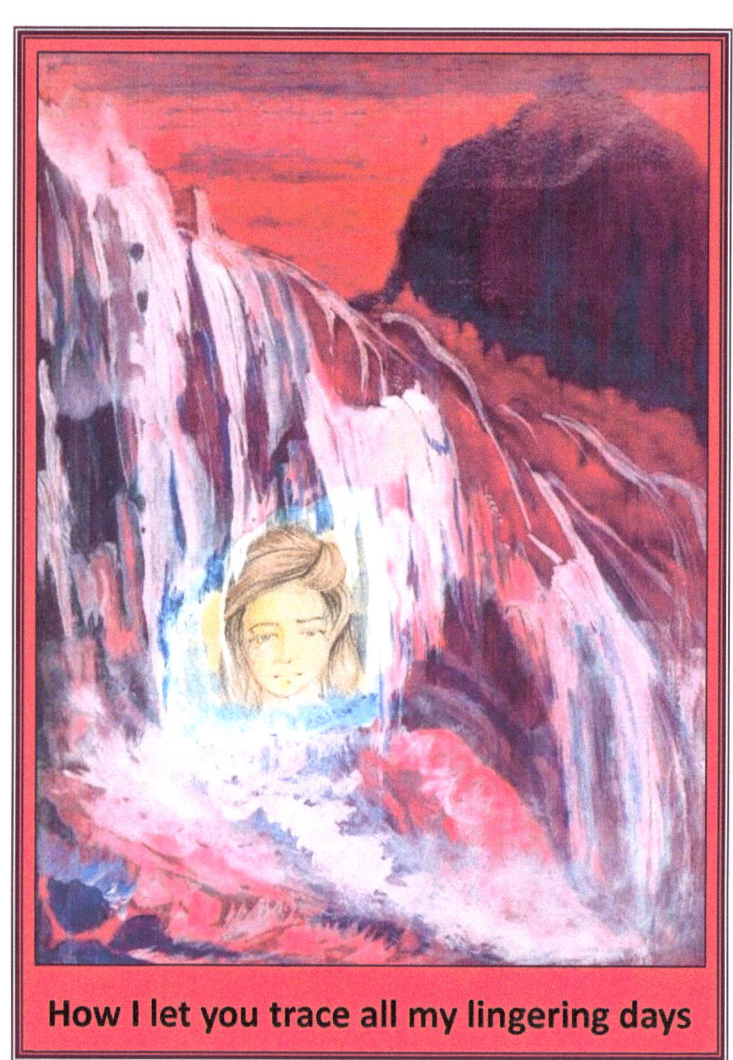

How I let you trace all my lingering days

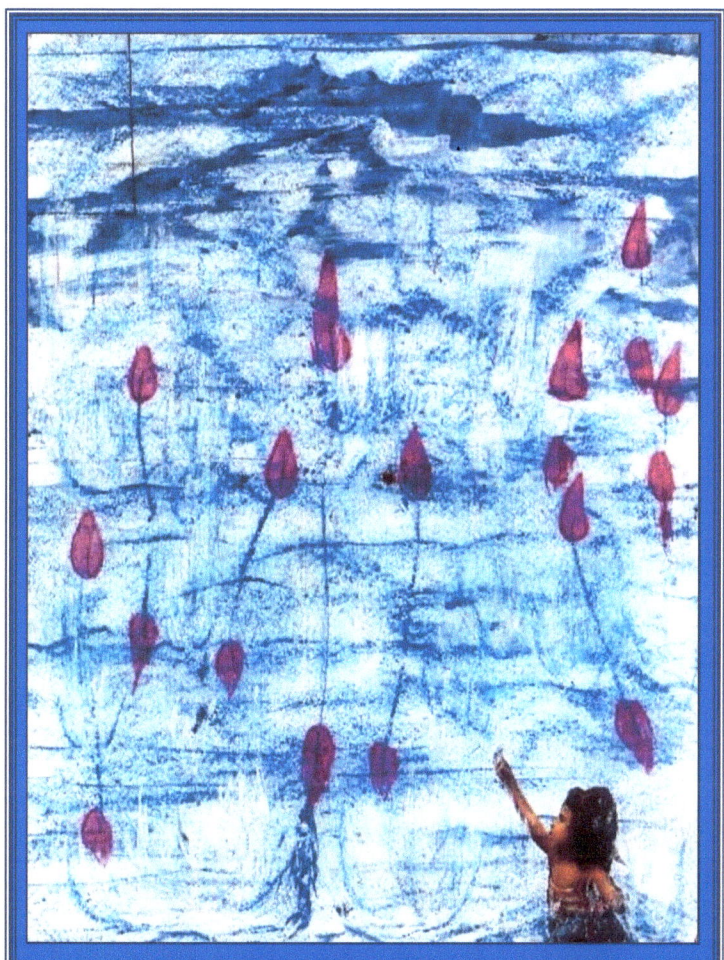

Life in Floating Leaves In my dreamy heaves

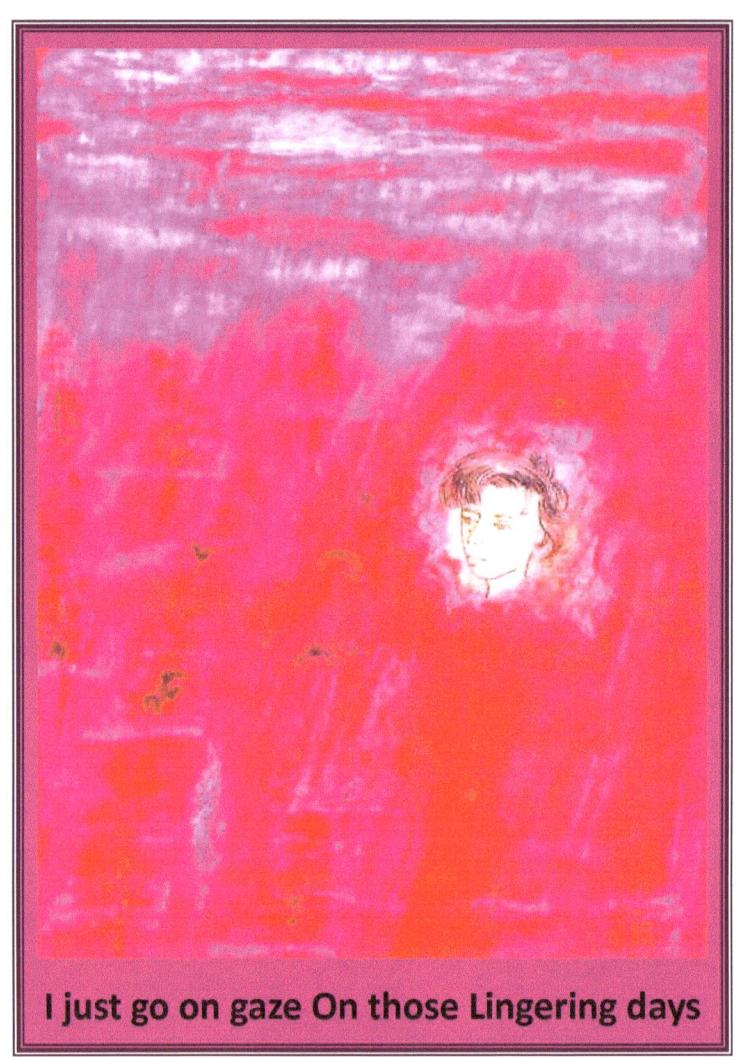

I just go on gaze On those Lingering days

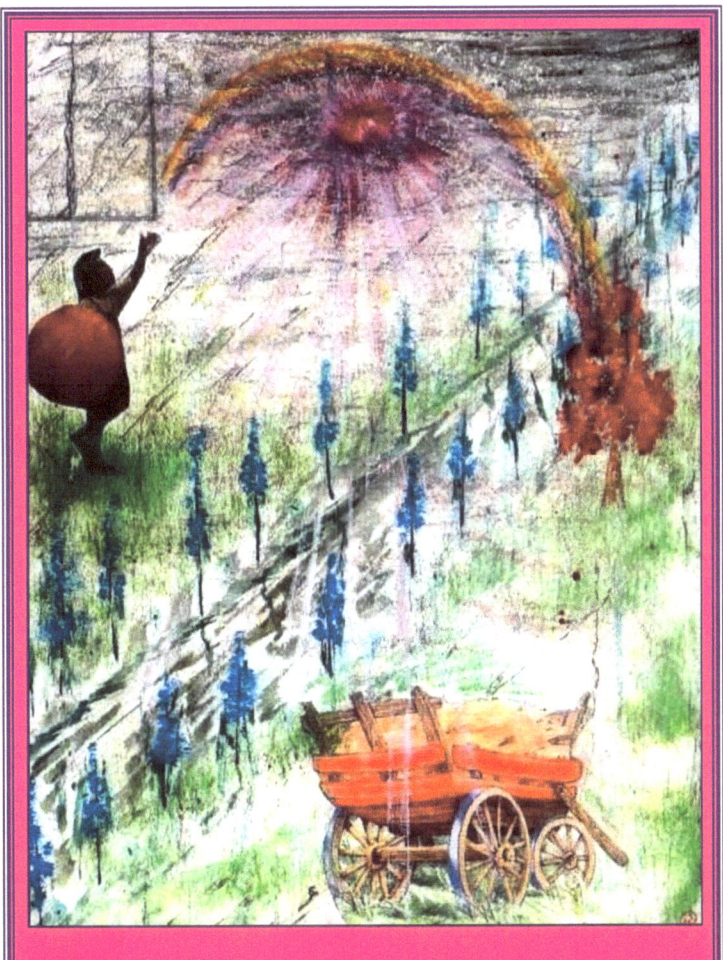

Can I forget Rains, Rainbow & Terrains

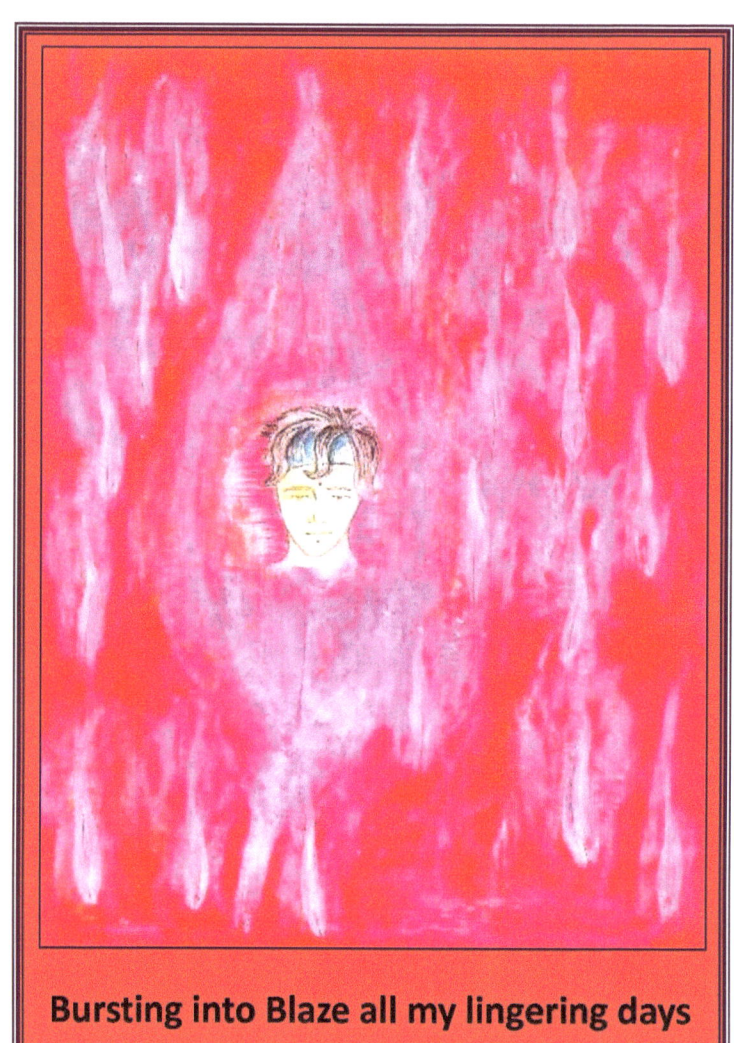

Bursting into Blaze all my lingering days

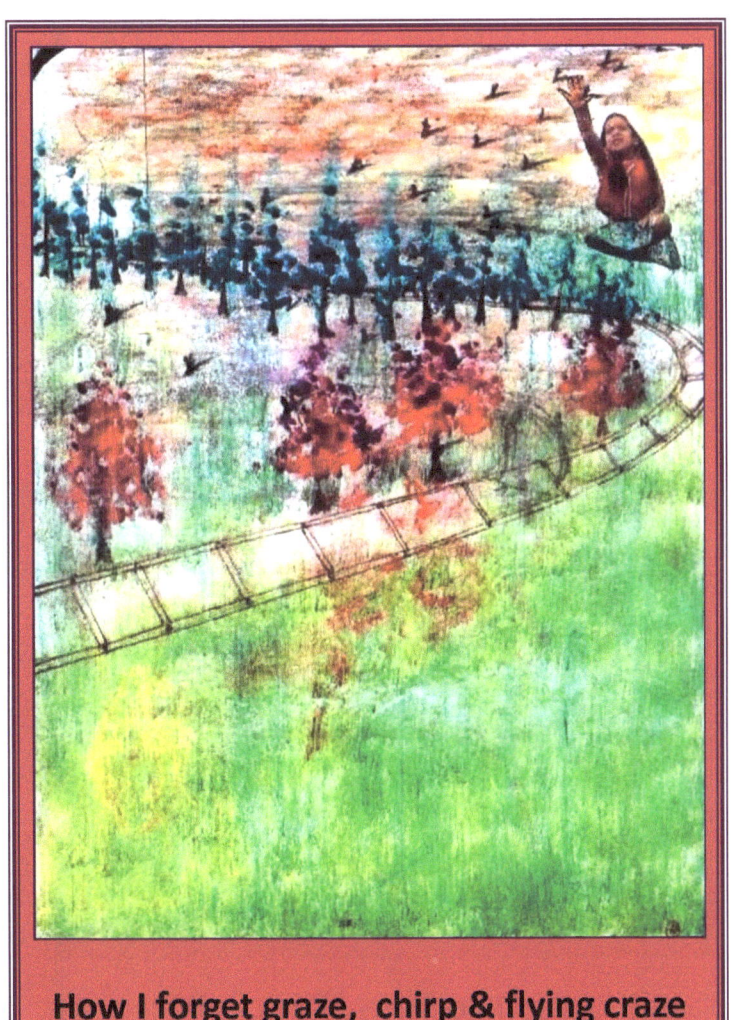

How I forget graze, chirp & flying craze

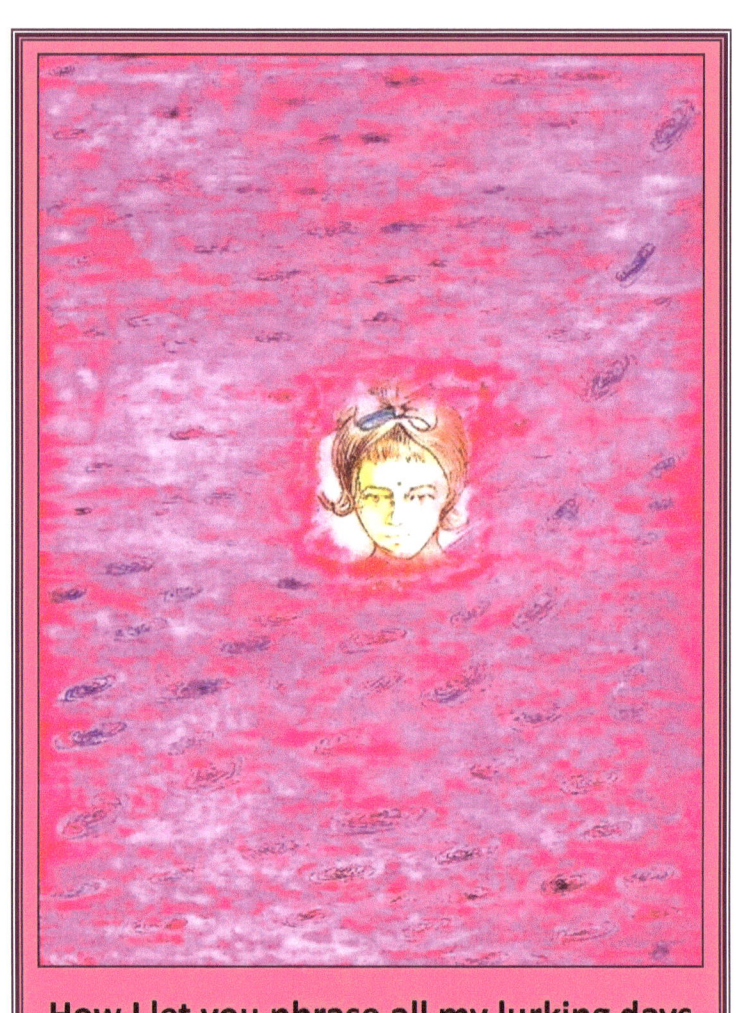

How I let you phrase all my lurking days

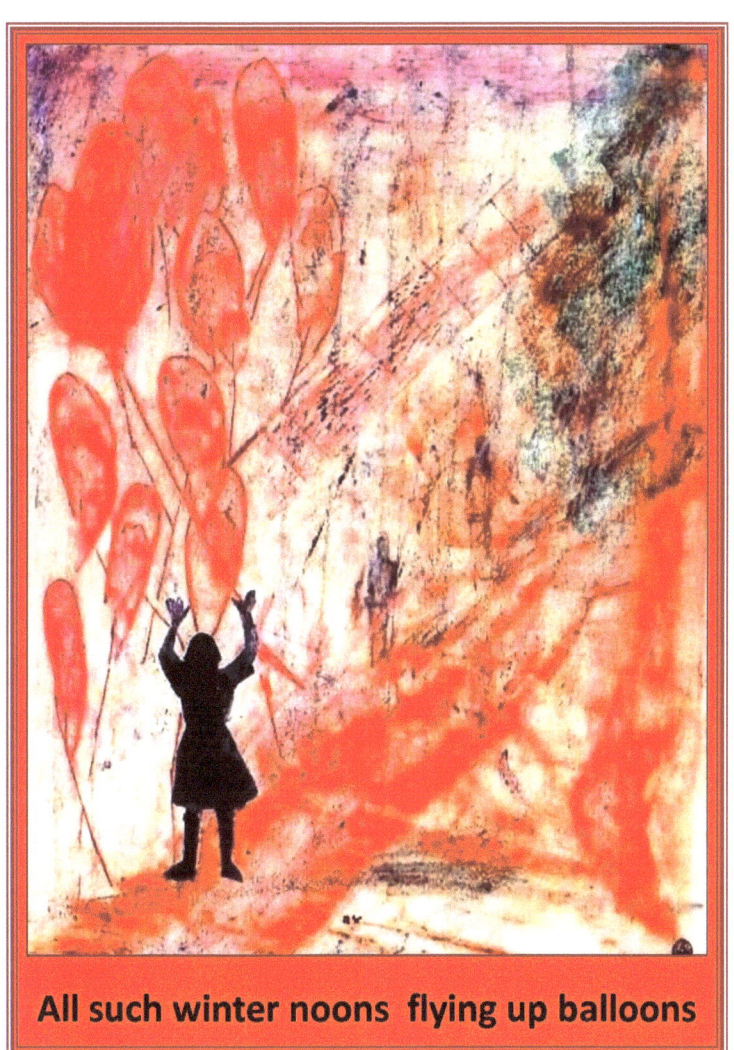

All such winter noons flying up balloons

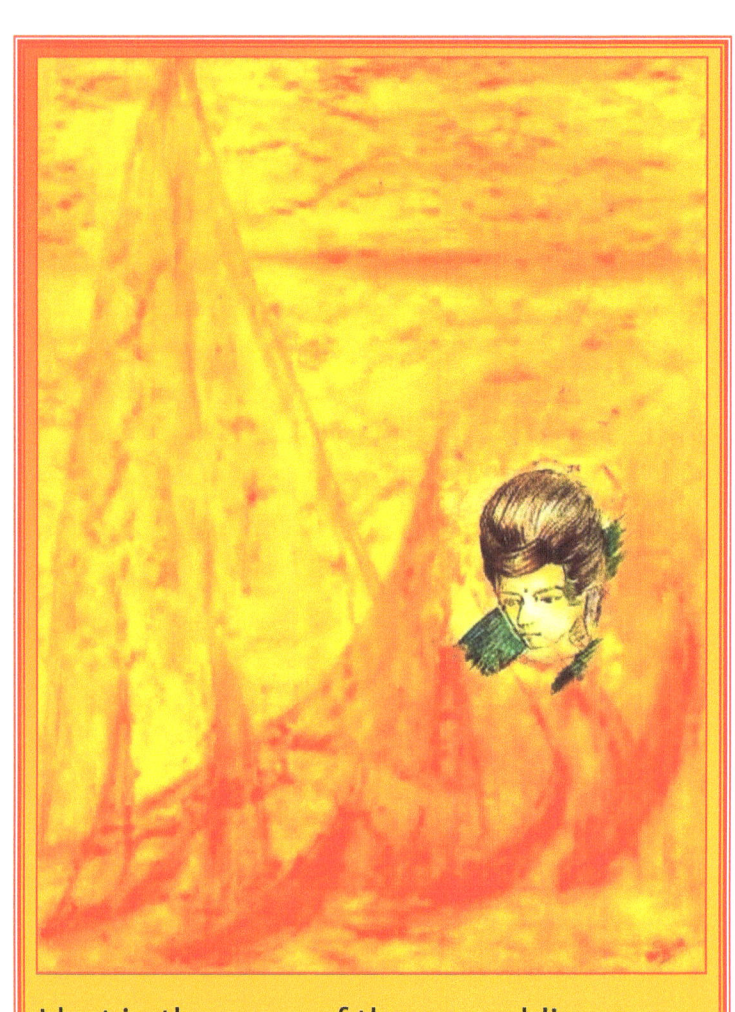

I lost in the maze of those rumbling waves

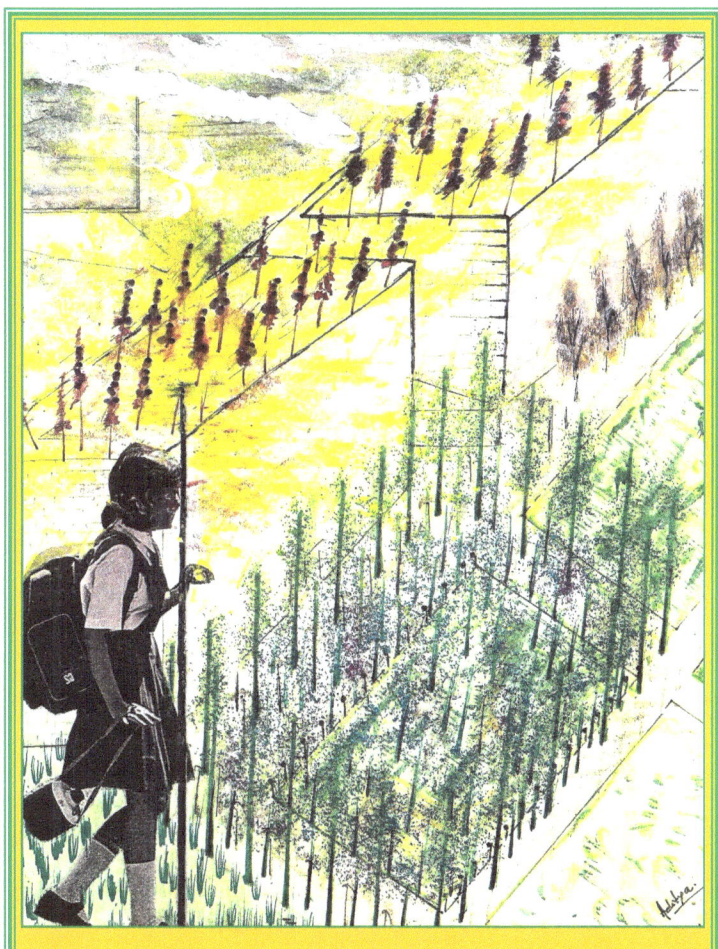

Swinging swirling pace on such windy days

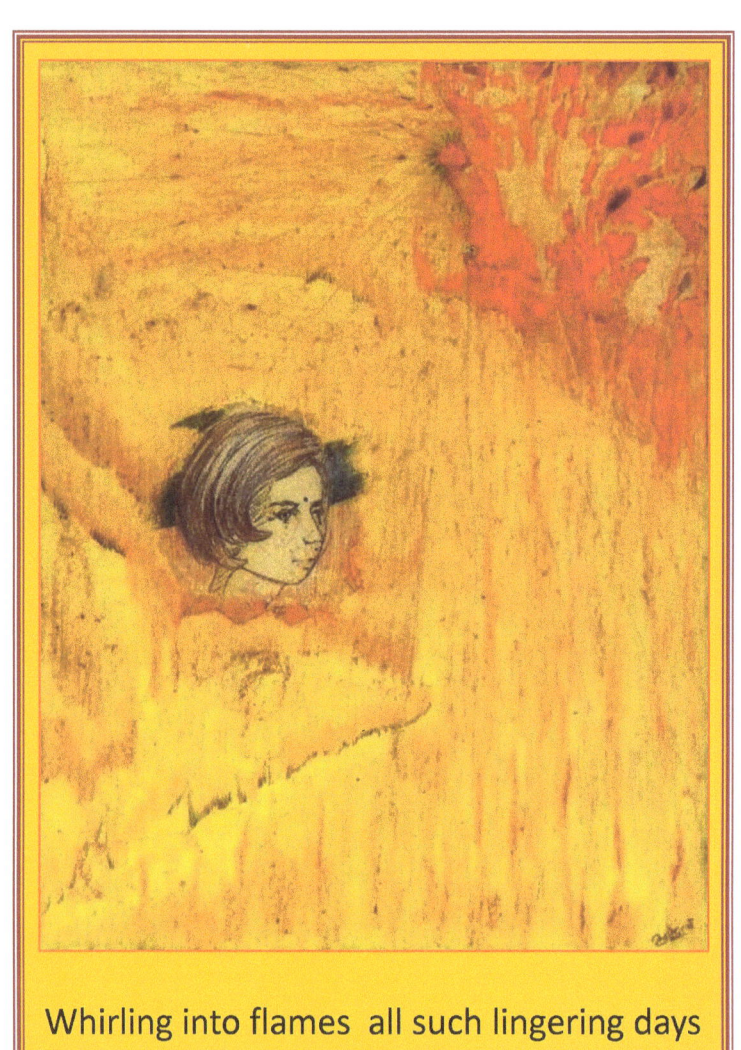

Whirling into flames all such lingering days

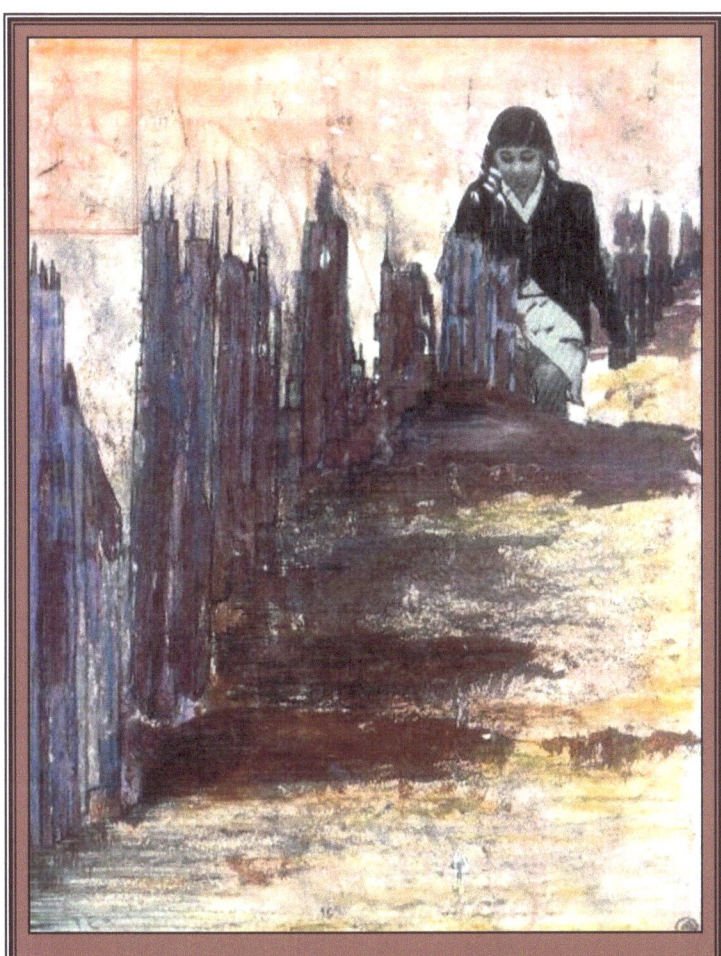

All such crush & plays , dark & daring days

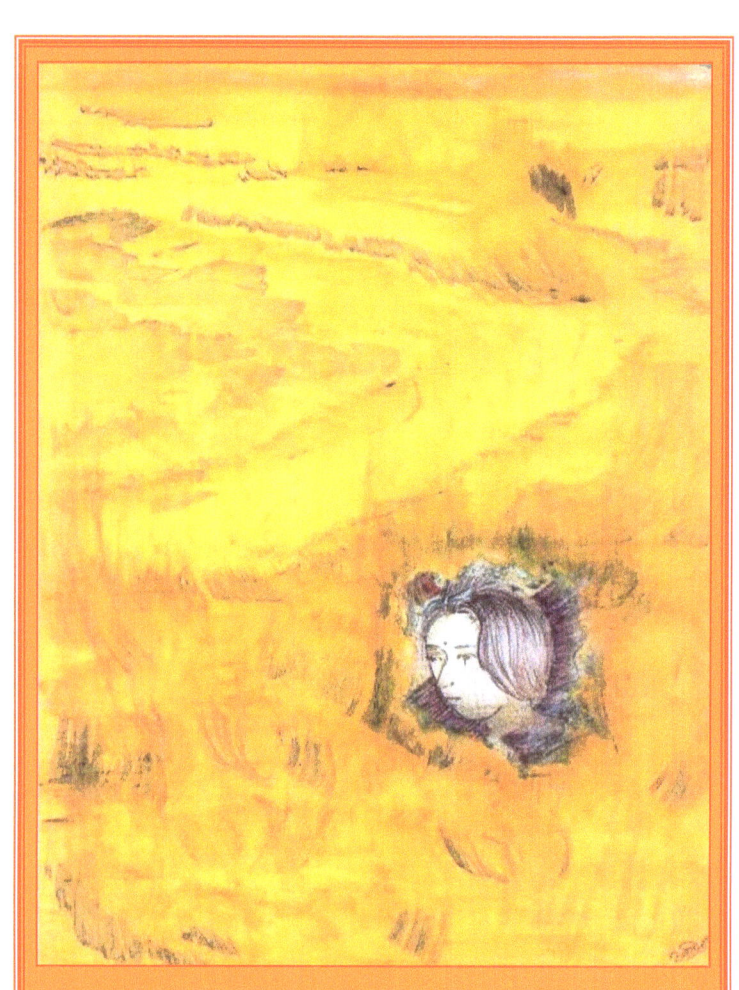

Loneliness embrace when I think those days

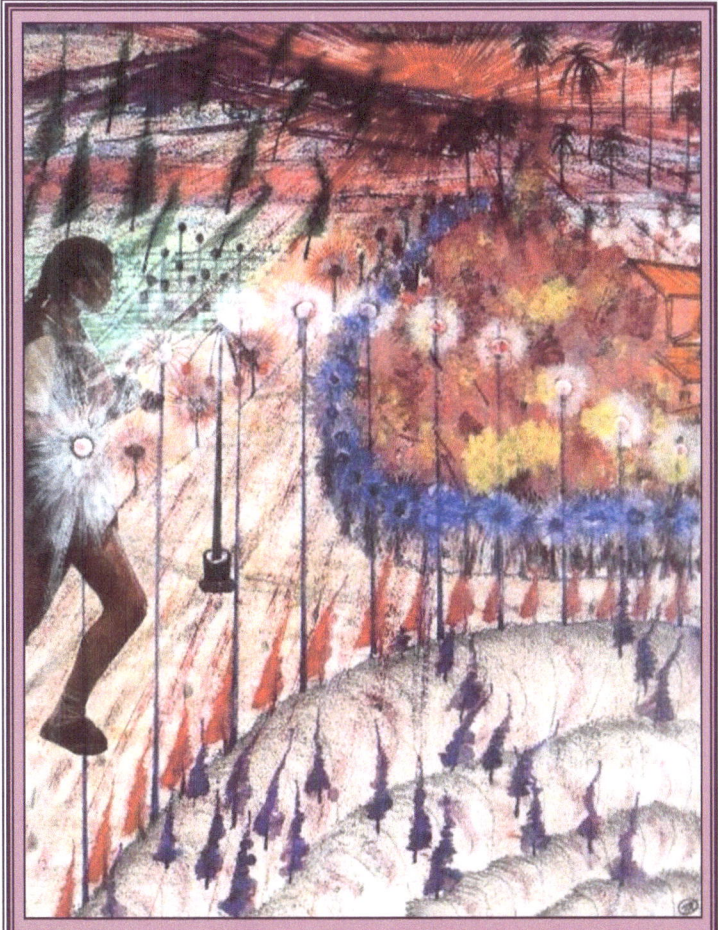

My crush, dress & dates jives & dancing days

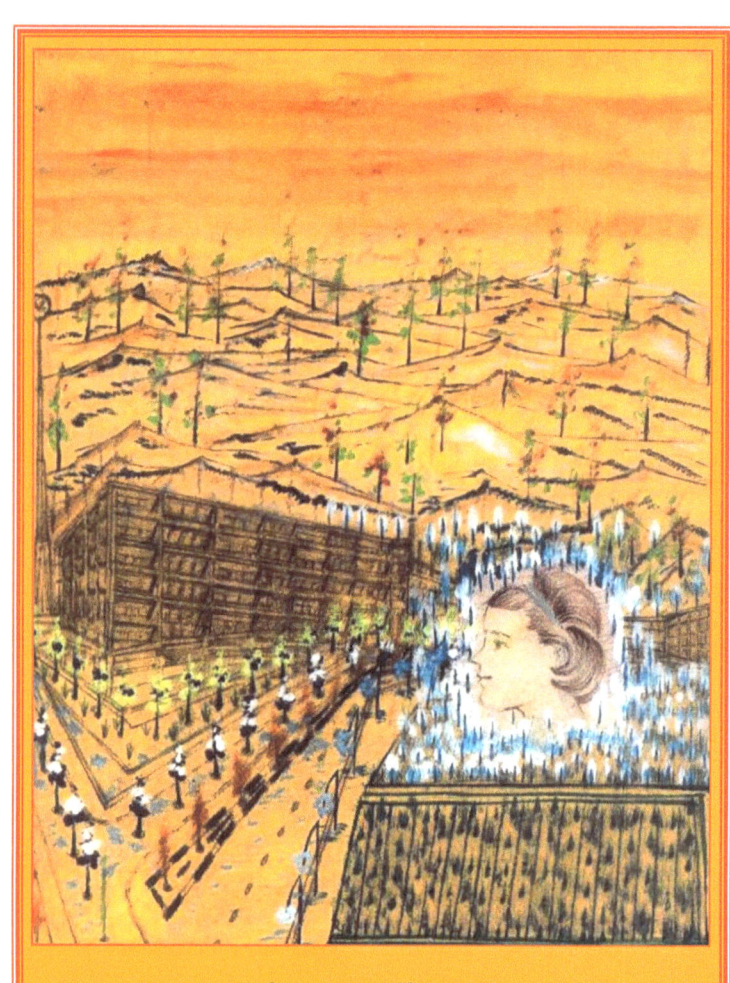

How I paraphrase all my happy days

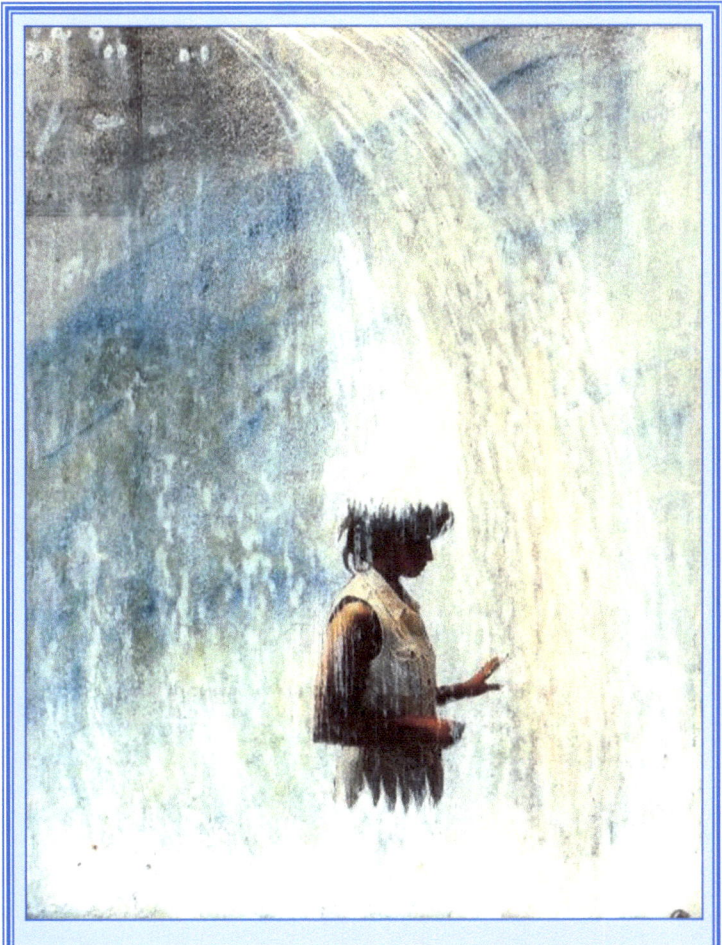

Dreams and fantasies , love and ecstasies

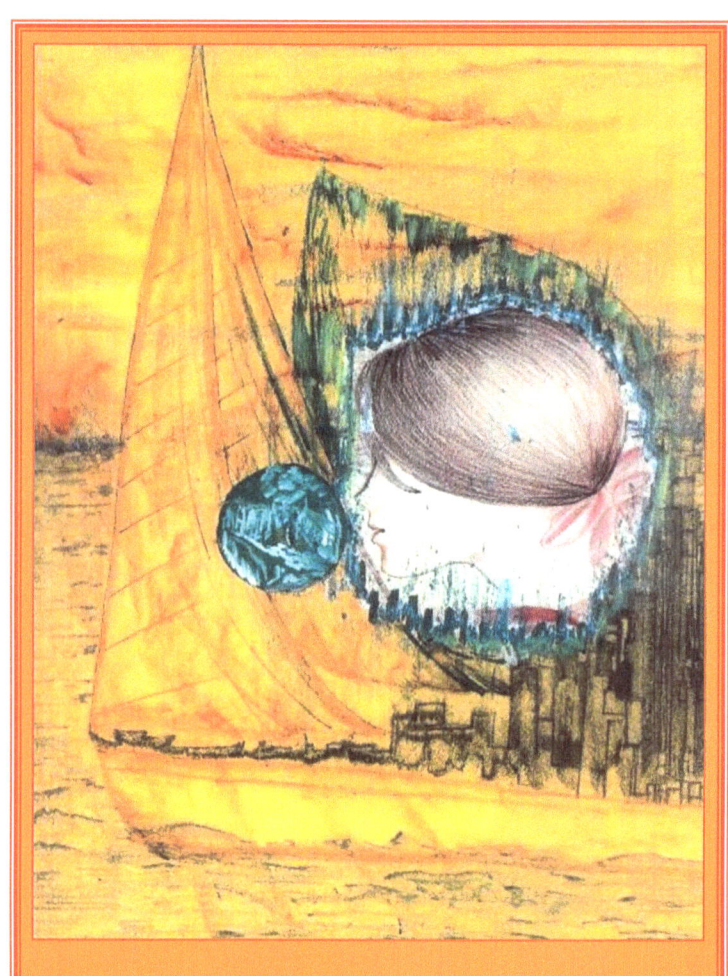

How I let you chase, journey night & days

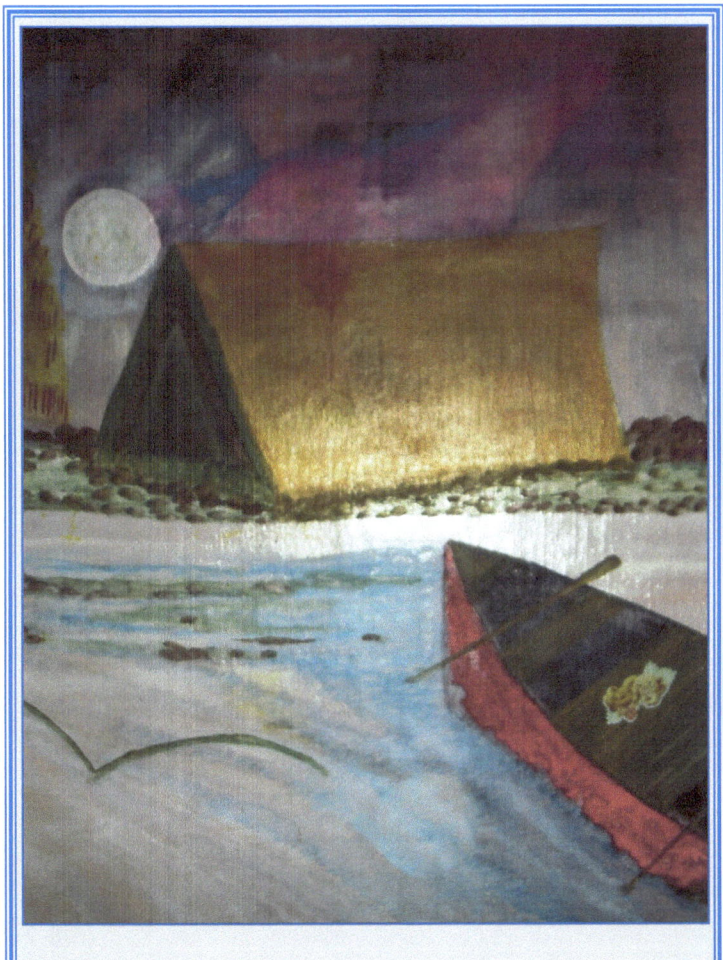

How I forget days love in Full moon rays

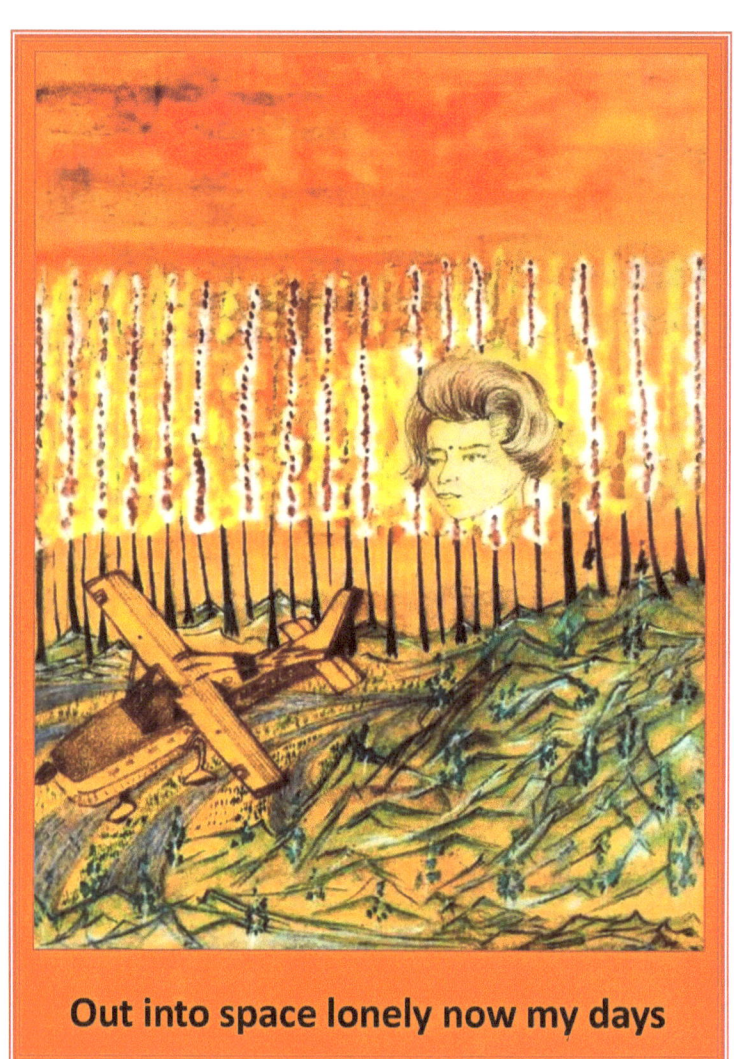

Out into space lonely now my days

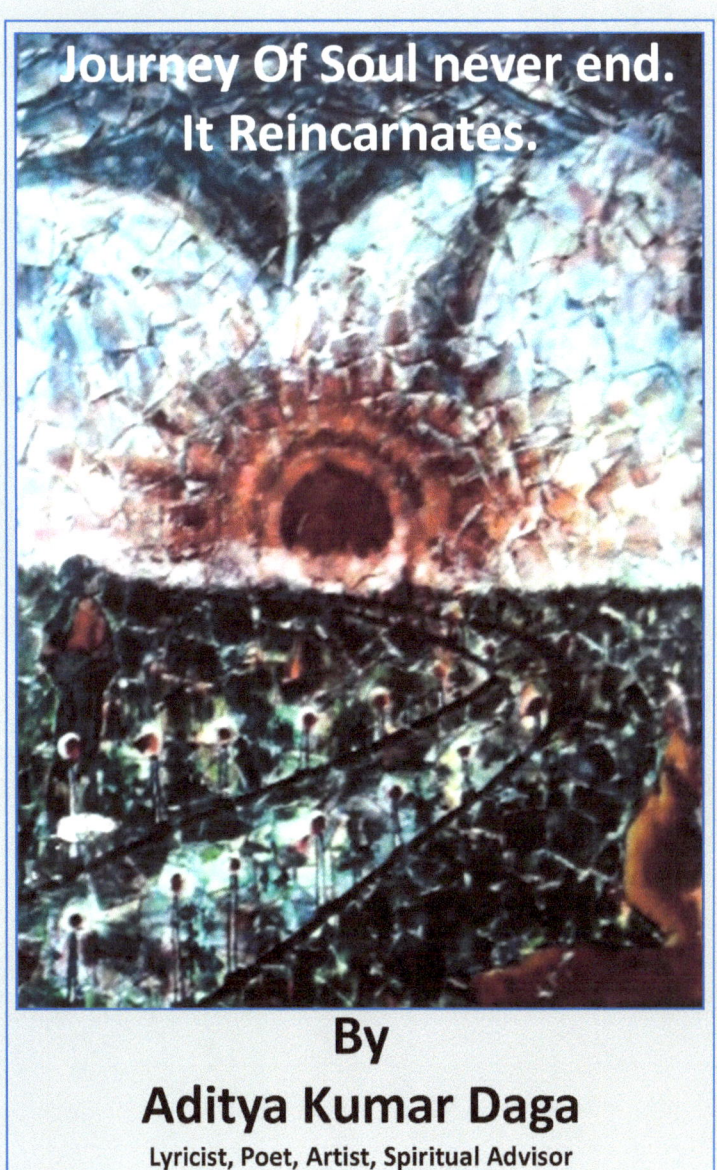

Journey Of Soul never end.
It Reincarnates.

By
Aditya Kumar Daga
Lyricist, Poet, Artist, Spiritual Advisor